Native Americans

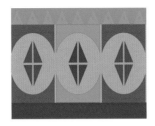

Mojave

Barbara A. Gray-Kanatiiosh

ABDO Publishing Company

visit us at
www.abdopub.com

Published by ABDO Publishing Company, 4940 Viking Drive, Suite 622, Edina, Minnesota 55435. Copyright © 2004 by Abdo Consulting Group, Inc. International copyrights reserved in all countries. No part of this book may be reproduced in any form without written permission from the publisher.

Printed in the United States.

Cover Photo: Stephan Trimble
Interior Photos: Corbis pp. 4, 28, 29, 30
Illustrations: David Kanietakeron Fadden pp. 7, 9, 11, 13, 15, 17, 19, 21, 23, 25, 27
Editors: Kate A. Conley, Jennifer R. Krueger, Kristin Van Cleaf
Art Direction & Maps: Neil Klinepier

Library of Congress Cataloging-in-Publication Data

Gray-Kanatiiosh, Barbara A., 1963-
   Mojave / Barbara A. Gray-Kanatiiosh.
     p. cm. -- (Native Americans)
   Includes bibliographical references and index.
   Contents: Where they lived -- Society -- Food -- Homes -- Clothing -- Crafts -- Family -- Children -- Myths -- War -- Contact with Europeans -- Famous leader -- The people today.
   ISBN 1-57765-936-8
   1. Mojave Indians--History--Juvenile literature. 2. Mojave Indians--Social life and customs--Juvenile literature.
[1. Mojave Indians. 2. Indians of North America--Arizona. 3. Indians of North America--California.] I. Title. II. Native Americans (Edina, Minn.)

E99.M77G69 2003
979.1004'9757--dc21
                                                                                    2003044318

About the Author: Barbara A. Gray-Kanatiiosh, JD

Barbara Gray-Kanatiiosh, JD, Ph.D. ABD, is an Akwesasne Mohawk. She resides at the Mohawk Nation and is of the Wolf Clan. She has a Juris Doctorate from Arizona State University, where she was one of the first recipients of ASU's special certificate in Indian Law. Barbara's Ph.D. is in Justice Studies at ASU. She is currently working on her dissertation, which concerns the impacts of environmental injustice on indigenous culture. Barbara works hard to educate children about Native Americans through her writing and Web site, where children may ask questions and receive a written response about the Haudenosaunee culture. The Web site is: www.peace4turtleisland.org

About the Illustrator: David Kanietakeron Fadden

David Kanietakeron Fadden is a member of the Akwesasne Mohawk Wolf Clan. His work has appeared in publications such as *Akwesasne Notes*, *Indian Time*, and the *Northeast Indian Quarterly*. Examples of his work have also appeared in various publications of the Six Nations Indian Museum in Onchiota, NY. His work has also appeared in "How the West Was Lost: Always the Enemy," produced by Gannett Production, which appeared on the Discovery Channel. David's work has been exhibited in Albany, NY; the Lake Placid Center for the Arts; Centre Strathearn in Montreal, Quebec; North Country Community College in Saranac Lake, NY; Paul Smith's College in Paul Smiths, NY; and at the Unison Arts & Learning Center in New Paltz, NY.

Contents

Where They Lived

The Mojave (mo-HAH-vee) called themselves the *Pipa Aha Macav*. In the Mojave language, *Pipa Aha Macav* means "people who live along the river." Their language was part of the Yuman language family.

The Mojave homelands included parts of present-day Arizona, California, and the southern tip of Nevada. Their neighbors included the Pima, Southern Paiute, Papago, Quechan, Hualapai, and Yavapai peoples.

The Mojave lived along the Colorado River. Their territory stretched from the Black Mountains to the Tyson Wash. They lived east of the Old Woman Mountains and west of the Hualapai Mountains.

The desert in Arizona near the Hualapai Mountains

These lands were harsh and **diverse**. They were made up of valleys, meadows, mountains, washes, rivers, and streams. In other areas lay mesas, dunes, and desert. Piñon trees, grasses, and berries grew in the valleys and mountains. Along the Colorado River grew cottonwoods, mesquite, **tule** (TOO-lee), willows, shrubs, and wildflowers.

Mojave Homelands

Society

Mojave society was divided into two bands. The northern band lived in the Mojave Valley, along the Colorado River. The southern band also lived along the Colorado River, but south of Chemehuevi Valley.

Each Mojave band further divided into smaller clusters of extended families. These clusters each lived in separate settlements. However, the Mojave bands quickly united when they needed to protect their people and land.

The Mojave believed dreams were powerful. People gathered to hear and interpret dreams. Leaders, medicine people, and warriors were chosen based on the dreams they had.

A head chief led each band. Each cluster of families also had chiefs and subchiefs whom the people respected. These chiefs led by moral influence rather than by force. Leaders gave speeches from the rooftops so that all the people could hear them.

Mojave society also had spiritual leaders. Festival chiefs were responsible for feasts and ceremonies. They also performed funerals, at which they gave speeches. Medicine people healed the Mojave. The dreams of the medicine people gave them the power to cure certain types of illnesses.

A Mojave man tells his dream to others in his band.

Food

The land provided the Mojave with the food they needed. The people hunted, fished, planted, and gathered. Mojave men hunted in the mountains for large game, such as deer. They also hunted rabbits, ground squirrels, birds, and lizards.

Most often, men hunted with lances or bows and arrows. However, the Mojave often caught smaller animals with handwoven snares and nets. They also hunted rabbits with curved throwing sticks that were similar to **Aboriginal** boomerangs.

Mojave men fished in the rivers. They often caught mullets, humpback suckers, and other fish. The Mojave caught these fish with hook and line, handwoven nets, weirs, traps, and canoe-shaped baskets. The people boiled the fish or cooked them on hot grills.

The Mojave planted their gardens in the Colorado River's floodplain. Each spring, melting snow in the north caused the river to flood. The floodwater left **sediment** on Mojave land, **enriching** the soil. After the floods ended, men and women planted their gardens in this fertile soil. They planted tepary beans, squashes, pumpkins, melons, and white corn.

Corn was an important source of food for the Mojave. The people husked the corn and placed it on the rooftops to dry. Once the corn was dried, they ground it into **meal**. They also ate roasted corn.

Women gathered wild seeds, cacti fruit, and desert plants. They also gathered mesquite beans, which they made into a sweet drink. Often, the Mojave dried some of their food. They stored dried corn, beans, and wild plants in **granaries** woven from arrowweed branches. The granaries protected the food from bugs, rodents, birds, and other animals.

A Mojave hunter readies his stick to throw at a rabbit.

9

Homes

The Mojave lived in two types of homes. During the hot summer, they slept under open-sided brush shelters. But in the winter, the Mojave lived in homes with walls.

The brush shelters, or ramadas, had frames of cottonwood poles. Across the top of the frame, the people laid arrowweed branches to form a flat roof. The sides of the shelter were left open. Inside, the people slept on woven mats.

Winter homes were rectangular with a sloped roof. The Mojave began building this type of home by digging a shallow, rectangular pit. Next, they stood a large, notched cottonwood pole on end at each corner of the pit. Then, they fit smaller cottonwood poles into the notches to create the frame and roof.

For the walls, the Mojave tied arrowweed branches to the frame. They tied mats to the roof with plant-fiber rope. Then, they covered the entire structure with several inches of grass, sand, and mud. This **insulated** the home and made it sturdy.

Mojave work and rest in
the shade of a ramada.

Clothing

The Mojave made their own clothing. Deerskin, rabbit skins, and woven plant fibers were common materials. Sometimes the Mojave decorated their clothing with **geometric** designs.

Mojave men wore long **breechcloths**. Women wore aprons and knee-length skirts. This handwoven clothing was made from the inner bark of willow trees.

Mojave women also wore beautiful beaded collars. One of these collars covered a woman's neck and upper body. Patterns of blue and white glass seed beads decorated the collar. The people received these beads and other items in trade with Europeans and other tribes.

Men and women wore woven corn husk sandals. They also made sandals from deerskin. In cold weather, the people wore woven rabbit fur capes and blankets. They often wore necklaces of shells and beads that they had received while trading with coastal tribes.

Mojave men and women put mud and mesquite bark shampoo in their hair to make it shiny and clean. Women grew their hair long and let it hang loosely. Mojave men wore their hair in rolls that looked like ropes. In this hairstyle, about 13 rolls hung down from the back of the head.

A Mojave woman and man wearing traditional clothing and body paint.

The Mojave also tattooed themselves. Both women and men tattooed their faces. Men did their bodies, too. The Mojave used charcoal for the tattoo dye. The tattoos were usually **geometric** designs of dots and lines.

The Mojave also painted their faces, arms, and legs. They mixed clay, plants, and ground minerals to make different colors.

13

Crafts

The Mojave created useful crafts. Items such as pottery and baskets had many everyday uses. For example, pots and baskets could hold water and store food.

Besides storing food, pots had other uses. Sometimes, the Mojave used pots to float small children across the river. The child rode safely in the pot while an adult swam behind.

Women wove watertight storage baskets. To do this, they wove strips of a tree's inner bark together. These baskets were used to hold cornmeal and beans, and to carry seeds.

Men wove special baskets and nets for fishing. To make baskets, they first wove willow sticks together with twine made of plant fiber. Next, they wove the sticks into a canoe-shaped basket about four feet (1 m) long. Then the men attached a long, wooden pole to the basket as a handle.

These types of baskets scooped up fish from deep pools in the river. The men then carried the fish back to the settlement in a different willow basket. This carrier looked like a badminton shuttlecock. Attaching a woven burden strap allowed the men to wear the basket on their back.

Mojave men carry fish back from the river in woven carriers.

Family

Mojave settlements consisted of many extended families. Each member helped with daily chores. Often, Mojave men and women worked together.

Planting was one of their shared chores. The men made holes in the soil with wedge-shaped sticks. Women followed closely behind the men, placing seeds in the holes.

Mojave men also made the tools that they commonly used. For example, they would roll plant fibers into twine. They wove this twine into long, rectangular fishing nets. The men weighed down the net's edges with stones to prevent the fish from escaping.

Elders also had a special role in the family. They helped interpret people's dreams. The Mojave believed that dreams foretold the future.

Opposite page: Mojave family members often helped tattoo each other's faces.

Children

The Mojave cared for their children and taught them useful skills. They carried their babies on woven **cradleboards**. The people used mesquite tree roots to make the U-shaped frame. They tied willow twigs onto the frame to finish the cradleboard.

Children learned by watching the adults. When they were old enough, the children helped with daily chores. One such chore was gathering cacti fruit. Mojave children used long poles to knock ripe fruit off tall saguaro cacti. Cacti fruit were a good source of vitamin C for the Mojave.

Music was also a part of a Mojave child's life. Mojave children learned to make rattles with pebbles and gourds. They poured the pebbles into a dried gourd. Then they put a wooden handle in the hole to seal it.

Pebbles for the rattles were hard to find, but they could be gathered from around anthills. The Mojave left a gift of food at the hills to thank the ants for the pebbles.

Mojave children learned to take only what they needed from nature. They knew it was important to protect the plants and animals. Children learned about the different plants that grew along the riverbank. Cattails and **tule** could be eaten, while willow and arrowweed were used to make baskets and clothing.

A Mojave boy reaches up to knock fruit from the top of a saguaro cactus.

Myths

Origin stories tell of how the land was shaped and how people came to this world. The following is one version of how the Mojave came to live alongside the Colorado River.

The Great Spirit had died. Mastamho, the Great Spirit's younger brother, went to Earth. When Mastamho arrived, he found the land and people half formed.

Mastamho took his willow walking stick and pushed it deep into the earth. When he pulled out the stick, water spewed from the hole. The water formed into the great Colorado River.

The water was filled with fish, geese, and other water animals. Mastamho's giant hands scooped up mud. He made banks to hold the water. He also made the mountains. He took seeds from his pocket and planted corn, melons, beans, and squashes.

Mastamho gave the Mojave people hands with fingers. He taught them how to use their hands to make pottery, baskets, tools, bows and arrows, and nets. He showed the people how to build homes.

Mastamho gave the Mojave the special power to dream. He told the people to listen to their dreams.

Mastamho pulls his staff from the earth, drawing out the waters of the Colorado River.

War

The Mojave rarely fought among themselves. To prevent disputes, they marked farming boundaries with mud and arrowweed poles. However, sometimes a flood would move the markers. So, arguments about boundaries sometimes caused the Mojave to fight each other.

Though fights among Mojave were uncommon, the Mojave often battled or raided neighboring tribes, such as the Pima and Papago. Although the Mojave lived in scattered settlements, they quickly united in times of war. Sometimes, the Quechan people would join the Mojave to fight against common enemies.

Mojave warriors wore either a handwoven cap or flicker feathers in their hair. They believed the feathers would protect them from harm. In battle, one man was selected to carry a feathered flagstaff. This man had no weapons. The Mojave believed their dreams protected him from injury in battle.

The Mojave also believed dreams gave them special powers to fight. Mojave warriors were fierce, fighting with bows and arrows. In close combat, they fought with small wooden war clubs. They painted these clubs black with red trimming.

Warriors brought dried meat and mesquite beans with them. They also carried a gourd in a net. The gourd held water and was stopped up with a wooden cork.

A Mojave man with bow, arrows, and war club

Contact with Europeans

In 1540, Antonio de Mendoza was the **viceroy** of New Spain. That year, he sent Francisco Vásquez de Coronado to explore north of the colony. He also hired navigator and explorer Hernando de Alarcón. Alarcón was to sail up the Gulf of California and support Coronado's expedition.

Alarcón missed meeting with Coronado. Instead, Alarcón became the first European to travel up the Colorado River. He called it *Río de Buena Guía*, which means "river of good guidance" in Spanish. The Mojave were visiting Quechan territory when Alarcón arrived there.

In the late 1500s, a Spanish explorer named Juan de Oñate set up a colony in New Mexico. In the 1600s, he left on a mission to explore westward. In 1604, Oñate met a group of Mojave where the Colorado River meets the Bill Williams River.

The next visitor to the area didn't come until the late 1700s. At that time, Father Francisco Garcés became the first Spaniard to visit Mojave homelands. He noticed the river's red color and

The Mojave meet a Spanish explorer.

so named it *Colorado*, which means "red" in Spanish. Red clay in the riverbed gave the water its reddish color.

Then, around 1820, trappers and mountain men began traveling through Mojave territory. European settlers looking for a route into California **trespassed** onto Mojave lands. Conflicts over lands began. In 1858, the Mojave attacked a wagon train of settlers passing through to California.

After a while, the U.S. government saw the Mojave attacks as a problem. In 1858, land surveyor Lieutenant Edward Beale suggested that the U.S. military build Fort Mojave to protect white settlers. The Mojave fought against the intrusion, and many were killed.

Cairook

Cairook was a respected Mojave leader. He was born around 1800. Cairook was tall, handsome, and strong.

When he was a young man, Cairook dreamed he would become a chief like his father. He worked hard to develop his leadership skills. Soon he had won the respect of his people and became subchief of his band. Eventually, Cairook became chief.

Cairook guided surveyors such as Lieutenant Amiel Whipple and Lieutenant Joseph C. Ives. He helped the men explore parts of Mojave homelands. Cairook knew the area well and was able to give them good advice.

Around 1858, tensions between the Mojave and white settlers and traders erupted. Soldiers were sent in to protect the U.S. settlers. To maintain peace, Cairook and some younger chiefs agreed to go with the military.

Cairook did not know the military's plan. The military wanted to control the Mojave by holding their chiefs **hostage**. After being held for a year, the Mojave chiefs decided they must escape.

Cairook overpowered the guards while the other chiefs escaped into the Colorado River. Cairook tried to escape, but he was stabbed with a bayonet. He died while trying to return to his band.

Chief Cairook

The Mojave Today

Today, there are an estimated 3,700 Mojave tribal members. The Mojave have **three federally recognized** reservations. These reservations are located in California, Arizona, and a small part of Nevada.

The Fort McDowell Reservation is located near Scottsdale, Arizona. The Fort Mojave and Colorado River Reservations lie along the Colorado River, within the Mojave's traditional homelands. The Mojave share these two reservations with other tribes. As a result, the Mojave live on the Colorado River Reservation with their former enemies, the Chemehuevi.

A Mojave woman holds her baby on a cradleboard.

A young Mojave girl in 1903 with her
face traditionally painted

The Mojave are working to protect their **culture**, the health of their people, and the environment. However, dams built on the Colorado River have changed the river's natural environment.

For example, the dams have changed the river's flood patterns. The dams and pollution **endanger** many native fish. This has led to changes in the Mojave's diet and **economy**. Those changes have led to an increase in health problems, such as diabetes.

The Mojave realize that saving their culture depends on protecting the environment. Today, they work to preserve the traditional practices that once kept the people spiritually and physically healthy.

A Mojave girl sits on her grandmother's lap.

Glossary

Aborigine - a native person from Australia.

breechcloth - a piece of hide or cloth, usually worn by men, that wraps between the legs and ties with a belt around the waist.

cradleboard - a flat board used to hold a baby. It could be carried on the mother's back or hung in a tree so that the baby could see what was going on.

culture - the customs, arts, and tools of a nation or people at a certain time.

diverse - composed of several distinct pieces or qualities.

economy - the way a nation uses its money, goods, and natural resources.

endanger - to put in danger of becoming extinct.

enrich - to add nutrients to soil, making it more fertile.

federal recognition - the U.S. government's recognition of a tribe as being an independent nation. The tribe is then eligible for special funding and for protection of its reservation lands.

geometric - made up of straight lines, circles, and other simple shapes.

granary - a storage place for harvested grain.

hostage - a person held captive by another person or group in order to make a deal with authorities.

insulate - to keep something from losing heat by lining it with material.

meal - coarsely ground seeds.

sediment - fine sand, clay, or soil carried by water that settles on the bottom of a river or lake.

trespass - to unlawfully enter another person's property.

tule - a type of reed that grows in wetlands. Tule is native to California.

viceroy - a governor that acts as a representative of a king or queen.

Web Sites

To learn more about the Mojave, visit ABDO Publishing Company on the World Wide Web at **www.abdopub.com**. Web sites about the Mojave are featured on our Book Links page. These links are routinely monitored and updated to provide the most current information available.

Index